SAN JOSE

SHARKS

JOAN ST. PETER

Published by Creative Education
123 South Broad Street, Mankato, Minnesota 56001
Creative Education is an impfint of The Creative Company

Designed by Rita Marshall
Cover Illustration by Rob Day

Photos by: Bruce Bennett Studios, Focus on Sports, Sports Photo Masters

Library of Congress Cataloging-in-Publication Data

St. Peter, Joan.
San Jose Sharks / Joan St. Peter.
p. cm. — (NHL Today)
ISBN 0-88682-744-2

1. San Jose Sharks (Hockey team)—History—Juvenile literature.
[1. San Jose Sharks (Hockey team)—History. 2. Hockey—History.]
I. Title. II. Series.

GV848.S26S76 1995   93-48450
796.962'64'0979474—dc20

123456

SHARK ATTACK AT THE COW PALACE

I t wasn't the Sharks' first regular-season game. It wasn't even the team's first home game. But it was a game the Sharks and their fans will always remember. It was the expansion team's first win—and it happened on home ice.

On October 8, 1991, just three games into the Sharks' inaugural year, San Jose goaltender Brian Hayward led his team onto the ice at the Cow Palace, a building that served as the team's temporary home for the first two seasons. After an impressive

Goaltender Brian Hayward recorded the Sharks' first win.

effort against the Calgary Flames during the first two periods, the Sharks found themselves tied with the Flames midway through the third period. In a move that foreshadowed Kelly Kisio's future role with the Sharks, the veteran center scored the winning goal with only 3:15 left on the game clock, giving the Sharks a 4-3 victory. Flames goaltender Rick Wamsley was the victim of the Sharks' first bite.

The Cow Palace erupted with excitement as the fans celebrated their team's victory, setting the pace for the tremendous fan support the Sharks would enjoy in the seasons ahead.

"There's no question that the most exciting moment of the season was skating off the ice after that first victory and hearing the roar of that Cow Palace crowd," Hayward commented later. "That was special."

Jeff Odgers scored his first NHL goal in November in a victory over the Islanders.

THE BAY AREA WAITS FOR HOCKEY

San Jose, the third largest city on the West Coast and the 11th largest city in the nation, has a population of about 800,000 people. It is the capital of Silicon Valley, a region known for its advanced technology. More than 2,600 high-technology companies in the area employ more than 250,000 people. The combination of the flourishing business atmosphere, the size of the city and the warm, pleasant climate marked San Jose as a prime location for an NHL franchise.

But professional hockey was no stranger to the area. Almost 65 years before the Sharks debuted in 1991, Oakland and San Francisco, along with Los Angeles and Hollywood, formed the California Hockey League. California's first professional league

Pat Falloon is the club's all-time leading scorer (page 7).

Pat MacLeod played in 37 games for the Sharks during his rookie season.

lasted only five seasons, dissolving in 1933. But professional hockey would return to the Bay Area some 30 years later with the area's first NHL franchise, the California Seals.

The Seals were part of the NHL's 1967 six-team expansion that doubled its size to 12 teams. Known as "the Great Expansion," it also included the Minnesota North Stars, the St. Louis Blues, the Philadelphia Flyers, the Los Angeles Kings and the Pittsburgh Penguins. Originally called the California Seals, the team's name was changed first to the Oakland Seals and then settled as the California Golden Seals. The team went through some tough times—including four owners in its first three seasons—until finally in 1977, after only nine years, the California Golden Seals moved to Cleveland, Ohio, where the team was renamed the Cleveland Barons. A short time later, with the Cleveland Barons and Minnesota North Stars both struggling financially, the NHL allowed the teams to merge; they would play in Minnesota.

In June 1991 the league's sixth expansion brought the NHL back to California's Bay Area. Ironically, many North Stars players formed the core of the expansion San Jose Sharks franchise through the league's dispersal draft. The California Golden Seals had come full circle.

THESE WERE NO "SCREAMING SQUIDS"

The San Jose Screaming Squids? How about the Golden Gaters or the Golden Skaters? From the Blades to the Waves, more than 2,300 different names came flooding in when the San Jose expansion team held a name-the-team contest. Breakers, Breeze,

Fog, Grizzlies, Knights, Red Woods and Sea Lions were among the many entries. But in the end, the team owners went with the name Sharks, mainly because the nearby Pacific Ocean is home to many different kinds of sharks. The name also captured the kind of hockey team its owners strived for: strong and determined.

Strong and determined also describes the Sharks' co-owners, brothers George and Gordon Gund. George, whose office is located in San Francisco, has taken a more active role in hockey. He plays the sport and is a member of many hockey organizations, including the U.S. Hockey Hall of Fame and the International Council for USA Hockey. Away from the sport, George's interests lie in the film industry and in art. His brother Gordon, headquartered in Princeton, New Jersey, is the president of Gund Investment Corporation and is also involved in real estate development on the West Coast. Gordon, who played college hockey at Harvard, was diagnosed with retinitis pigmentosa, a disease that results in the loss of vision. He has been recognized nationally for his participation in charitable and philanthropic endeavors in the fight against the disease.

George Kingston was named head coach on April 12 and served for the first two seasons.

The Gunds' hockey involvement spans nearly two decades, including their first NHL endeavor, the Cleveland Barons. After taking control of the financially burdened Barons in 1977, the Gunds spearheaded the merger that united their team with the Minnesota North Stars. In that process, the Gunds took control of the North Stars and their home arena, the Metropolitan Sports Center (known as Met Center) in Bloomington, Minnesota. After 13 years of both successes and failures with the Minnesota franchise, the Gunds sold the North Stars in exchange for the rights to the San Jose expansion team.

Doug Wilson was captain for the first two seasons (pages 10-11).

San Jose welcomed their new team, selling out all 40 home games during their first season.

The Gunds hired Art Savage as president and Jack Ferreira as the team's general manager. George Kingston signed on as head coach. Dean Lombardi and Chuck Grillo completed the makeup of the team's administrative department. As general manager, Ferreira led the staff in building the new team. Through three drafts—the dispersal draft, the expansion draft and the entry draft—and various trades, Ferreira attempted to form a team of young and old, with an eye to both the present and the future of the franchise.

Captain Doug Wilson, a 14-year veteran of the NHL, proved to be a strong player who provided the character and leader-

ship the team needed to make it through a very difficult first year. Kelly Kisio, seasoned 11 years in the NHL, demonstrated heart and desire and provided a valuable example for the franchise.

Youthful talent sprinkled the Sharks' roster. Players such as J.F. Quintin, Pat MacLeod, Pat Falloon and Claudio Scremin were used sparingly, in hopes of giving them experience without burdening them with the pressure of the team's high expectations. Others, such as defensemen Neil Wilkinson and Rob Zettler, were young, too, but saw a lot of action on the ice because the team relied on their talents.

After a year of drafts, trades and preparation, it was time for the Sharks to sink or swim. Armed with experienced veterans, skilled young players and strong goaltending, the Sharks were set to begin their first season of play. It was what Ferreira called a "long-awaited moment" as a new era of NHL hockey began.

On October 4, Craig Coxe scored the Sharks' first goal on assists from Pavelich and Wilkinson.

An Uphill Battle

On October 4, 1991, San Jose played its first NHL game against the Canucks at the Vancouver Coliseum. The contest gave a glimpse of both the work ethic and the frustration that became a trademark of the Sharks' first two seasons. The Sharks fell behind early and appeared destined to lose their first game. Left winger Craig Coxe finally scored the franchise's first goal 4:09 into the third period. The goal lit a fire under the Sharks, and rookie defenseman Pat MacLeod tied the game, pumping in two goals in his first NHL game. The teams remained deadlocked until, with only 29 seconds remaining, Canucks captain Trevor Linden tallied the winning goal to defeat the Sharks 4-3.

In the Sharks' first season, Rob Zettler played in 74 games, scoring one goal and eight assists.

Although their first game didn't end with the thrill of victory, the Sharks' performance was encouraging. Their second game brought them back to San Jose for their home opener. Pregame festivities included a laser light show and tuxedo-clad ushers to welcome the sellout crowd of 10,888 eager fans. The Sharks lost that game, but their first win was right around the corner. Two days later, the Sharks beat their division-rival Calgary Flames in a 4-3 victory.

The season took a turn for the worse after the team's first win. The Sharks endured a 13-game winless streak on a two-week road trip before posting their next victory. But the excitement of the team's second win did not last. Over the following months the Sharks struggled, trying to match the level of competition they faced. Their first season concluded with a dismal record of 17 wins, 58 losses and 5 ties.

After the final game of the Sharks' disappointing first season, coach George Kingston met with the media and summed up the year on a positive note. "There aren't too many players who have taken a night off. . . . Assessing the overall year, I'm proud of the team."

One of those players who hadn't taken a night off, defenseman Neil Wilkinson, said confidently, "We came through it, and that's something no one can take from us."

The highlights of the Sharks' first season were the individual successes of the players. During that year, 19 rookies sported a Sharks jersey at one time or another. These players were brought up from the organization's farm team, the Kansas City Blades. Led by coach Kevin Constantine, the 1992 Kansas City Blades won the International Hockey League's Turner Cup, a minor league

J. F. Quintin played for the champion Kansas City Blades.

trophy similar to the NHL's Stanley Cup. That year, the Blades posted professional hockey's best record, winning 68 games while losing 25 and tying four.

How could the Sharks, parent club of such a skilled farm team, post such a mediocre record during the same season? The answer is that the team was building for the future. Many of the players who contributed to Kansas City's success during the 1991–92 season brought their offensive skills to the Sharks in the following years. And more players from that team are expected to lead the Sharks in the future.

Doug Zmolek was one of only five NHL rookies to play in every game in 1992-93.

Neil Wilkinson finished his first season in San Jose with 19 points and 107 penalty minutes. 17

Kelly Kisio scored 617 points in his eleven year NHL career.

But it was the near future—the team's second season—that produced more growing pains than the first, both on and off the ice. Off the ice, front-office turmoil sent general manager Ferreira packing after one season. Three vice presidents took control of what is usually handled by just one general manager. Vice president of hockey operations Dean Lombardi, vice president of player personnel Chuck Grillo and head coach George Kingston formed the first NHL front-office "triad."

On the ice, the Sharks' second season proved another frustrating year for the team. The year started out on a hopeful note with an exciting overtime win against the Winnipeg Jets at the Cow Palace, but then the Sharks suffered through long stretches without a triumph. Plagued with problems and injuries, the

Sharks hit their low point in January. A 4-1 loss to the Montreal Canadiens on January 4, 1993, started a 17-game losing streak for San Jose. The number matched the NHL's record for futility set by the 1974–75 Washington Capitals. In the entire 1992–93 season, San Jose recorded only 11 victories—six fewer than its first season. The fallout from that dismal performance included the firing of coach Kingston in the summer of 1993. He was replaced by Kevin Constantine, who was brought up from the Kansas City Blades. Sharks fans hoped that he could do for the Sharks what he did for the Blades. He didn't disappoint them.

Kelly Kisio scored a goal and an assist in the 1993 All-Star Game.

HOPE FOR THE FUTURE

"Our first few years were key as we obtained players through the entry draft," Dean Lombardi said in the summer of 1993. "Our average roster age is under 25 years old and will likely get even younger in the next year or two. We have many exciting, talented young players on the horizon who will be the core of our team for many years to come."

Developing their young players' leadership qualities has been an important part of the Sharks' growth process. The first two years the Sharks were led by key veteran players, and one in particular—Kelly Kisio. "His play has been outstanding—he was our team MVP in 1992–93, tying his career high in goals (26) and points (78)," Lombardi said. "His leadership abilities are important to the Sharks both on and off the ice." Kisio has been with the Sharks since the beginning and earned his fins as a captain.

The team's overall offense was showing signs of improvement, aided by the addition of Rob Gaudreau and the maturing of young

21

Pat Falloon quickly became a standout player.

Pat Falloon. Falloon was the Sharks' first draft selection in 1991, second overall. His potential became reality much sooner than anyone expected when Falloon led the team in all offensive categories as a 19-year-old rookie. Named to the NHL's All-Rookie team, he ranked among the top five NHL rookies in points, goals and assists. He finished fourth in the NHL rookie-of-the-year voting. Falloon quickly became one of the Sharks' most popular players as home-ice fans chanted "Falooooooooon" whenever his stick touched the puck. In his second season, Falloon was selected to play in the NHL All-Star Game, but an injury forced him to miss the game and the final three months of the season. Falloon has established himself as a pivotal member of the Sharks.

Sandy Ozolinsh set a Shark record for most points (64) in a season by a defenseman.

Several other Sharks, all defensemen, have been raising their games to a new level. "Sandis Ozolinsh from Latvia is one of our very skilled youngsters on defense. On the way to that position is Mike Rathje, a 6-foot-5 junior star who was our first pick in 1992," observed Lombardi.

Ozolinsh played a big part in the Kansas City Blades' Turner Cup championship in 1992. He graduated to the NHL in 1992–93 and led the Sharks' defense in scoring, despite missing the last half of the season with a knee injury. In 1993–94, he positioned himself among the league's best, ranking 11th overall in scoring and fourth on the Sharks' roster. Rathje, the Sharks' 1992 first-round draft pick, third overall, saw limited time, playing in 47 games, but is expected to improve the Sharks' defense in the near future, along with Michal Sykora.

After finishing at the bottom of the standings for two seasons, the Sharks finally began to see dividends during the 1993–94 campaign—and then some. Rookie coach Kevin Constantine and the

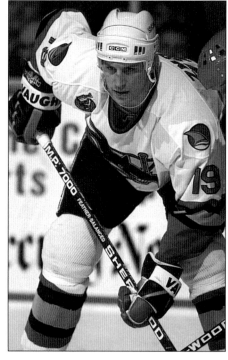

24   *Left to right: Ulf Dahlen, Brian Hayward, Kelly Kisio, Doug Zmolek.*

Sharks made waves around the NHL by producing the greatest single-season turnaround in NHL history. San Jose improved 82 points from the previous season with a 33-35-16 record. The Sharks' memorable year was capped with a third-place regular-season finish in the Pacific Division and the team's first playoff berth, which brought them to within one game of the Stanley Cup semifinals.

Igor Larionov had the best plus-minus record for the Sharks with a +20.

The Sharks' thrilling accomplishments brought Constantine runner-up honors for the Jack Adams Award as coach of the year. Goaltender Arturs Irbe established himself as one of the league's best goaltenders with a 2.84 goals-against average in 71 games. New acquisitions Ulf Dahlen and Todd Elik injected character, offense and leadership into the lineup. The Sharks' defense was a definite bright spot and should only get better in the years to come.

With a few seasons under their belts, the Sharks appear to be heading in the right direction.

BEHIND THE SHARKS

"It's been great being in on the ground floor of a franchise, seeing the excitement for our team and the sport," said Sharks center Kelly Kisio. He also appreciates the Bay Area location. "It's a beautiful part of the country where there are so many things to do away from the rink. It's helped me adjust both on and off the ice."

In an area of warm temperatures, sandy beaches and 300 sunny days a year, the Sharks organization works hard to educate Bay Area fans—especially kids—about the game of ice hockey and

Rob Gaudreau is a tough, consistent competitor (pages 26-27).

to carve a niche for themselves in the market. Because there is little ice in sunny California, the Sharks took to the streets with their "Sharks and Parks" program. "Sharks and Parks teaches children the basics of hockey through street hockey as well as providing a healthy activity for the kids," explained Sharks president Art Savage. "We've found that the best way to educate people is get them to witness the sport itself."

S. J. Sharkie helped cheer the Sharks to a winning record at home during their third season.

The team also offers hockey camps during the offseason to educate fans. Although handling only ice hockey, the camps accommodate kids of all skill and age levels.

Another teacher of the game is actually a member of the shark family. But this shark was not discovered by the team's scouting staff, nor does it live in the ocean. It is known as S.J. Sharkie. Born in a hockey arena that uses a Zamboni machine with a fin, S.J. Sharkie was adopted as the Sharks' mascot in January 1992. He was officially named on April 15, 1992. To celebrate his identity, S.J. Sharkie made national headlines—and a big splash—by bungee jumping from the Cow Palace rafters.

These days, S.J. Sharkie can bungee jump from the rafters of the Sharks' brand-new building, the San Jose Arena. Located in downtown San Jose, the arena is designed specifically for hockey. Its 18,000 seats give it one of the largest arena capacities in the NHL.

Even though the team struggled on the ice and played in a temporary home for two seasons, the popularity and marketing success of the Sharks has been second to none. Fans all over the country are going "Pacific teal." The team logo, featuring the shark and an extraordinarily popular color scheme—Pacific teal, black and white—launched the Sharks' merchandise pop-

Right wing Sergei Makarov led the club with 30 goals in 1993-94.   29